Original title:
Lullabies Under the Lunar Glow

Copyright © 2024 Creative Arts Management OÜ
All rights reserved.

Author: Sophia Kingsley
ISBN HARDBACK: 978-9916-90-678-1
ISBN PAPERBACK: 978-9916-90-679-8

Verses of Dreaming Souls

In the hush of night we wander,
Seeking whispers, soft and tender.
Stars above in gentle light,
Guide our dreams until the night.

Waves of thought in silent streams,
Float away like fleeting dreams.
Time stands still, no need to rush,
In this moment, feel the hush.

Hearts entwined in soft embrace,
Lost within this sacred space.
Every heartbeat, every sigh,
In our dreams, we learn to fly.

Awake we may, but still we know,
In our souls, the dreamers glow.
Here we dance, both free and bold,
In the night, our dreams unfold.

Embracing Stars in Evening's Calm

Underneath the velvet sky,
Whispers of the night breeze sigh.
Stars are twinkling, hearts aligned,
In their glow, our souls unwind.

Every twinkle tells a tale,
Of our dreams that dared to sail.
Holding tight, we feel the spark,
Guiding us within the dark.

Night unveils its silver cloak,
In this hush, we softly spoke.
Wrapped in warmth, the world unfolds,
Wonders waiting to be told.

As we share a timeless glance,
In the night, we find our chance.
Embracing stars, we come alive,
In evening's calm, our spirits thrive.

Songs of the Veiled Moon

Under the silver veil, whispers sing,
Secrets of dusk in soft winds cling.
Shadows dance lightly on paths unknown,
Guided by light, we wander alone.

Branches sway gently with tales untold,
Crickets compose hymns, the night unfolds.
Stars blink above in a cosmic embrace,
Echoes of laughter, a tender trace.

Breaths of the Night's Tranquility

In the cradle of night, silence sleeps,
Moonlight weaves dreams, as darkness keeps.
The world holds its breath, time stands still,
As twilight whispers, hearts gently thrill.

Soft are the murmurs that float through the air,
A moment of peace, heavy with care.
Velvet shadows creep, yet kindness glows,
In the stillness of night, serenity flows.

Celestial Canopies and Comforting Verse

Beneath canopies where starlight spills,
Songs of the heavens softly fulfill.
Each twinkle, a promise, a warm embrace,
In the quiet of night, we find our place.

The tapestry woven with shimmering threads,
Dreams lightly dance where the moonbeam spreads.
With every breath drawn through night's gentle veil,
Hope is a lantern, love will prevail.

Stars and Dreams in Cosmic Harmony

In the vast expanse where stardust sways,
Dreams find a rhythm in cosmic ballet.
Galaxies spin as the night sings sweet,
Each heartbeat echoes where two worlds meet.

Let wishes take flight on the wings of the night,
Guided by hope, shining ever so bright.
In the embrace of the infinite skies,
We become starlight, where every dream lies.

Chamber of Soft Celestial Dreams

In twilight's embrace we softly drift,
Where shadows dance and secrets lift.
A cradle woven in silver light,
Guides our thoughts into the night.

With every sigh, the stars align,
Whispers of fate in gentle twine.
A lullaby from realms unseen,
Wraps our hearts in calm serene.

Through window panes, the moonlight streams,
Filling the air with tender dreams.
Each star a wish, a hope so bright,
In this chamber, we take flight.

Let the night unfold its grace,
In this sacred, timeless space.
Together we find solace deep,
In soft celestial dreams, we sleep.

Moonlit Reflections and Gentle Rest

The moonlight casts a silver glow,
On tranquil waters, soft and slow.
Ripples echo the night's sweet hymn,
As we find peace, our worries dim.

Stars above hold stories rare,
Glimmers flashing in the air.
We breathe in deep, the stillness sings,
In this moment, our spirits take wings.

A silent dance of shadows play,
Guiding lost souls along the way.
In nature's arms, we gently sway,
Night's embrace, a soft ballet.

With every heartbeat, dreams unfold,
In whispers of dusk, by night consoled.
Under moonlit skies, we rest our heads,
In serene reflections, love spreads.

Night's Cradle of Whispering Dreams

Within the cradle of night's keep,
Listen closely, the stars softly weep.
With every twinkle, secrets shared,
In whispered tones, they've always cared.

The velvet sky, a blanket wide,
Holding our wishes close inside.
A tapestry of light and shade,
Where fragile hopes are gently laid.

Dreams take flight on silent wings,
Carried forth on night's sweet strings.
In this haven, hearts convene,
Lost in night's soft, tranquil scene.

Wrap us in your quiet embrace,
Guide us with your tender grace.
In night's cradle, we find our way,
To whispered dreams that softly sway.

A Serenade of Stars and Softness

Stars awaken the silent night,
Casting wishes, pure and bright.
With every flicker, whispers say,
The magic of night will light our way.

In shadows deep where secrets lie,
We dance beneath the velvet sky.
Each note a dream, each breath a song,
In this serenade, we all belong.

Softness wraps us in its charm,
Keeping us safe, away from harm.
In gentle rhythms our hearts align,
With the universe, a love divine.

As dawn approaches, shadows fade,
Yet in our hearts, the dreams are laid.
A serenade of stars held near,
In whispers soft, we hold it dear.

Celestial Nights and Dreamy Light

Stars twinkle softly in the dark,
Whispers of magic spark the heart.
Moonbeams dance on velvet skies,
Guiding dreams where silence lies.

Clouds drift lazily in gentle sighs,
A lullaby sung where the night flies.
In this realm where wishes flow,
The universe wraps us, warm and slow.

Galaxies swirl in a cosmic dance,
Promising hope with each fleeting glance.
Night's embrace, a tender flight,
Cradles us in celestial light.

When Shadows Weave Sweet Dreams

When shadows weave through the night,
Gently casting a tender sight.
Dreams unfurl like petals wide,
In the stillness where we bide.

Echoes of laughter fill the air,
As whispered secrets take us there.
Each heartbeat sings of calm delight,
Guided by the moon so bright.

Close your eyes, let worries flee,
In this moment, just be free.
Under starlit canopies above,
We find solace in a world of love.

Glimmers of Twilight and Lunar Embrace

Glimmers of twilight paint the sky,
As day bids farewell with a sigh.
The sun sinks low, fading from sight,
While the moon rises, a beacon of light.

Branches sway in the gentle breeze,
Nature whispers, urging us to seize.
Every shadow tells a tale,
Of lonely hearts that will not pale.

In lunar embrace, we feel it near,
The magic of night, serene and clear.
A tapestry woven with threads of gold,
Stories of dreams yet to unfold.

A Ballet of Stardust and Sleep

A ballet of stardust fills the night,
With twirls and spins, a graceful flight.
Sleep's gentle call lulls us near,
In a world where worries disappear.

Each twinkle tells of a dream unwound,
As night's embrace softly surrounds.
Floating on clouds of silken grace,
We journey through time and space.

The rhythm of slumber sings anew,
As celestial wonders come into view.
With every heartbeat, the cosmos hums,
In this dance of night, our spirit comes.

Hush of the Stars' Embrace

In silken night, the stars align,
Whispers soft, a sigh divine.
Moonbeams kiss the earth below,
In this hush, our hopes will grow.

A gentle breeze sings through the trees,
Carrying secrets on the ease.
In every shadow, dreams take flight,
Wrapped in cloaks of silver light.

The cosmos twinkles, a timeless dance,
Inviting souls to share a chance.
With every pulse, the night reveals,
A world where only silence heals.

In this embrace, we find our home,
A sanctuary, where far we roam.
Under starlit skies, we dwell,
In a whisper only time can tell.

Moonlit Melodies of Solace

Beneath the moon, a melody plays,
Softly guiding the night's ballet.
Each note carries a gentle stream,
Weaving through our midair dream.

The shadows dance on silvered ground,
Where echoes of sweet solace sound.
Every heart beat, a rhythmic sway,
In this soft serenade, we stay.

Stars above join in the song,
In unity, we all belong.
The night unfolds its tender grace,
In moonlit arms, we find our place.

Every whisper of the breeze,
Brings comfort like the rustling trees.
Together in this tranquil air,
We lose ourselves without a care.

Dreamweaver's Twilight Chorus

In twilight's glow, the dreams arise,
Weaving tales beneath soft skies.
Flutters of hope in every shade,
In the stillness, fears do fade.

Faint whispers of a nightingale,
Carry stories in the vale.
A chorus sings in harmonious flight,
Guiding wanderers through the night.

With every breath, the world ignites,
In starlit splendor, hearts take flights.
Each moment stitched within the night,
A tapestry of pure delight.

Dreamweaver spins with tender hands,
Crafting futures where love expands.
In this chorus, we find our way,
To brighter tomorrows, come what may.

Gentle Rhythms of the Night Breeze

The night breeze flows with gentle grace,
Caressing shadows, a soft embrace.
Each breath of air a soothing balm,
In its rhythm, the world is calm.

Under the cloak of velvet skies,
The stars awaken, brightly rise.
In tranquil murmurs, secrets shared,
Through whispered winds, we are ensnared.

Each rustling leaf, a voice of lore,
Echoing tales from times of yore.
As night unfolds its fragrant song,
In its cradle, we all belong.

Bound by the magic of the night,
We dance beneath the silver light.
Together, hearts in harmony,
In gentle rhythms, wild and free.

The Moon's Whisper to Sleeping Souls

In shadows deep, the moonlit gleams,
Whispering secrets, soft as dreams.
Sleepy eyes and breath so light,
The world fades softly into night.

Crickets sing a lullaby sweet,
While stars above begin to meet.
Night drapes gently, a silken shawl,
Embracing the silence, enfolding all.

The breeze conveys the moon's soft sigh,
As dreamers wander, floating high.
Lost in visions, they drift away,
To where the night holds sway.

From slumber's grasp, the whispers soar,
Inviting souls to explore once more.
In the quiet, the heart finds peace,
In moon's embrace, sweet troubles cease.

Nightfall's Gentle Serenade

The sun dips low, the sky ablaze,
Night unfurls in tender ways.
Softly hums a distant tune,
As starlight dances with the moon.

Beneath a blanket, crisp and bright,
The world is wrapped in velvet night.
Gentle whispers, the trees respond,
A serenade, a soothing bond.

Shadows flicker, memories play,
While dreams unfold without delay.
Each heartbeat syncs with night's refrain,
A soft embrace, a warm domain.

Nightfall beckons, come take a chance,
In twilight's glow, let spirits dance.
Leave behind the day's rough shore,
In nighttime's arms, we dream once more.

Stardust Cradle and Dreaming Heart

In stardust cradle, dreams take flight,
Kissed by whispers of the night.
The universe, a sparkling sea,
Embraces all who dare to be.

Through cosmic rivers, we will sail,
Where wishes ride on every trail.
Each heart aglow, with stories told,
In silver beams, our dreams unfold.

As gentle winds begin to weave,
Tales of wonder, we believe.
In distant lands, our spirits roam,
Each star a guide, a path to home.

In every flicker, hope resides,
As dreams awaken, the heart abides.
Cradled softly, we find our part,
In stardust's embrace, a dreaming heart.

Melodies of the Midnight Glow

The clock strikes twelve, the world sleeps tight,
But melodies linger in the night.
A symphony of silence flows,
In harmony where stillness grows.

The moonlight dances, shadows play,
On gentle hills where nightbirds sway.
Their songs entwined with softest sighs,
In whispered notes, the spirit flies.

Each star a note, each wish a dream,
In midnight's glow, all fears redeem.
Together with the night we weave,
A tapestry of hopes, believe.

As dawn approaches, the music fades,
Yet in our hearts, the echo stays.
In every moment, the glow will last,
The melodies of night are vast.

Serenades from the Deep Blue Night

The stars they twinkle in the dark,
As whispers float on evening's lark.
A serenade of waves and breeze,
Night's symphony brings hearts to ease.

The moonlight paints the ocean's crest,
In silver tones, a gentle rest.
Each note softens the world's fierce cry,
As shadows dance and dreams take flight.

The Moon's Lull of Dreams and Wonder

Beneath the tapestry of night,
The moon hums sweetly, pure delight.
It cradles dreams with tender grace,
In its embrace, we find our place.

With stardust thoughts that softly glow,
The mind can wander, drift, and flow.
A lullaby spun from the skies,
Where wishes whisper, softly rise.

Cradled in Night's Gentle Arms

The night wraps all in velvet calm,
Each shadow sings a soothing psalm.
The world outside begins to fade,
In twilight's hue, peace is laid.

Stars emerge in sparkling rows,
As moonbeams dance on silent throes.
Cradled close in night's embrace,
We find solace in this space.

Evoke the Stars' Soft Glow

In the stillness of the night,
Stars awaken, shining bright.
Their soft glow, a gentle kiss,
Invites the heart to dream in bliss.

Echoes of the cosmos sing,
As night unfolds its magic wing.
To evoke the calm above,
Is to feel the universe's love.

Serenade from the Starry Skies

In the hush of night, stars gleam bright,
Whispers of love take their flight.
The moon casts shadows, soft and light,
Holding secrets, hidden from sight.

With every note that the wind plays,
Hearts entwined in a gentle haze.
Nature sings in a wondrous praise,
Bound by the magic of starry days.

Nocturnal Melodies of Serenity

Creatures stir in the calm delight,
Melodies weave through the cool night light.
Shimmering leaves dance in the breeze,
Nature's symphony brings sweet ease.

Echoes blend in a lullaby tune,
Under the watch of the silver moon.
With each heartbeat, the night draws near,
Filling our hearts with tranquil cheer.

Cradle Songs Beneath Celestial Beams

In shadows deep, dreams softly play,
Cradle songs bring the dusk to stay.
Under stars that twinkle so bold,
Ancient tales of love unfold.

Hushed whispers ride on the night air,
Carried by hope, free from despair.
The universe sings with a sigh,
While the world beneath quietly lies.

Moonlight Dreams and Starlit Sighs

Moonlight spills on the path we roam,
Guiding our thoughts as we wander home.
Starlit sighs echo deep within,
A promise of peace where love begins.

Each beam glimmers, tales left untold,
With wishes scattered like grains of gold.
Together we breathe in the night's embrace,
Finding our place in a timeless space.

Starlit Cradlesong Serenade

In the hush of night, whispers sway,
Twinkling dreams hold children at play.
Moonlight dances, shadows softly creep,
Starlit lullabies, guiding to sleep.

Gentle breezes, secrets in their flight,
Cradling hearts beneath the silver light.
With every heartbeat, the universe sings,
Enchanting tales that hope brings.

Softly wrapped in twilight's gaze,
Every moment, a timeless maze.
Through the silence, a promise unfurled,
In starlit cradles, a melody swirled.

As stars awaken in the velvet sky,
Peaceful wishes on the wind will fly.
Embraced by dreams, in slumber we stay,
In starlit cradles, forever we'll play.

Silvery Echoes of Nighttime

Silvery echoes dance across the air,
Moonlight glimmers, a silken layer.
Whispers of night, secrets softly told,
In the stillness, their magic unfolds.

Each star a hymn, a note in the night,
Guiding our hearts with gentle light.
The night beholds a shimmering grace,
In every corner, a tranquil place.

Crickets sing with a rhythmic heart,
Nature's chorus, a symphonic part.
In shadows deep, where dreams reside,
Silvery echoes become our guide.

As dawn approaches, the echoes fade,
Yet in our hearts, their memory stayed.
A serenade of moonlit grace,
Silvery echoes, our solace in space.

Night's Embrace: A Gentle Requiem

Night's embrace, a soft-spun shroud,
Whispers of memory, echoing loud.
Tears of stars through the velvet sky,
A gentle requiem, a lullaby.

In twilight's grasp, we find our calm,
Nature's heartbeat, a soothing balm.
Each sighing breeze, a tender sigh,
Carrying hopes as the moments fly.

Time suspends in starlit grace,
As dreams unravel in a sacred space.
What once was lost, found in the dark,
Requiem of night, a tender spark.

As sleep descends with a velvet touch,
We cradle our sorrows, not so much.
In night's embrace, we find release,
A gentle requiem, a song of peace.

Celestial Cradle of Peace

In the celestial cradle, we softly sway,
Wrapped in moonlight at the end of the day.
Stars above whisper tales of old,
A tapestry woven with threads of gold.

Clouds drift slowly, like dreams in flight,
Embracing the world in the arms of night.
Each breath a promise, tender and sweet,
In this cradle, we find our retreat.

The universe cradles our hopes alive,
Within this peace, our spirits thrive.
Serenity blooms in the quiet space,
The celestial cradle, a warm embrace.

As dawn approaches, the sky turns pink,
In this moment, we pause and think.
Celestial wonders, our hearts release,
Forever anchored in this cradle of peace.

Fables Under the Starlit Sky

Whispers of the night take flight,
Tales of dreams in silver light.
Creatures dance through shadows deep,
Secrets wrapped in silence keep.

In moonlit glades where fairies play,
Lost in myths that twilight sway.
Stars compose their celestial songs,
Echoing where the heart belongs.

As lanterns glow on ancient trees,
Stories float upon the breeze.
Hushed each heartbeat, breathless sigh,
Fables weaving, you and I.

Underneath this cosmic dome,
All our fables find a home.
Each glance shared, a woven thread,
In starlit dreams, our spirits fled.

Moonlit Boughs and Gentle Tunes

Branches sway in softest breeze,
A serenade among the trees.
Moonlight glimmers on the stream,
Nature hums, a tender dream.

In twilight mist, the shadows weave,
Melodies that hearts believe.
Crickets chirp in choir's blend,
Each note a lover's gentle send.

Stars align in rhythmic grace,
Embracing every hidden space.
With every rustle, nature's sigh,
Stirs the whispers of the high.

Gathered 'neath this silver glow,
We find harmony in flow.
Bonded by the night's embrace,
Together, lost in time and space.

Enigmas of the Sleepy Universe

Galaxies whisper secrets deep,
In the heart of cosmic sleep.
Dreams unfold in colors bright,
A tapestry of endless night.

Constellations weave their spells,
Ancient stories they can tell.
Eclipses lend a shadow's grace,
Life unfolds in quiet space.

Planets spin in silent dance,
Each a world in fateful chance.
In the stillness, wonder blooms,
Enigmas rise like autumn's plumes.

Beyond the veil of starry skies,
Mysteries where magic lies.
In every twinkle, truths emerge,
From slumber's depths, the cosmos surge.

Caresses from the Night's Veil

Softly wrapped in darkness, tight,
The gentle caress of the night.
Stars like candles flicker bright,
Guiding dreams with tender light.

The moon bestows a silken touch,
Whispering secrets, oh so much.
In shadows deep, the spirits rise,
Painting wishes 'cross the skies.

Every sigh a breeze's kiss,
In this moment, find your bliss.
With every star, a promise made,
As night enfolds, fears will fade.

Crickets sing a soothing tune,
Beneath the watchful, silver moon.
Caresses from the night's own heart,
Binding souls that shan't depart.

Twilight Embrace of Distant Stars

The sky blushes soft, a gentle hue,
Where light meets shadow, night is anew.
Stars awaken, twinkling bright,
Whispering secrets, hidden from sight.

In the hush of dusk, dreams take their flight,
Embraced by whispers, soft as the night.
With each heartbeat, the cosmos unfolds,
Tales of forgotten, longing and bold.

Beneath the canopy, our spirits roam,
Guided by starlight, we find our home.
In twilight's embrace, we are set free,
Carried by wishes, like leaves on the sea.

The universe dances, a radiant glance,
In the twilight embrace, we dare to prance.
Lost in the magic, together we sway,
Under the blanket of the Milky Way.

Starlit Whispers Beneath the Sky

Beneath a tapestry of shimmering light,
We share our dreams, in the still of night.
Each star a promise, a tale to unfold,
In whispers so soft, like secrets retold.

The moon spills silver on the world below,
Illuminating paths where gentle breezes flow.
With every breath, the night hums a tune,
A lullaby woven with the heart of June.

Under the vastness, our worries take flight,
In starlit whispers, we gather our might.
Together we journey through shadows and beams,
Finding our solace in the depth of dreams.

Each twinkle a moment, a memory clear,
Guiding our souls to the things we hold dear.
In the dance of the night, we trust and we sigh,
Embraced by the whispers beneath the sky.

The Moon's Gentle Song

The moon hums softly, a lullaby pure,
Wrapping the world in a silvery lure.
With each gentle note, the night finds its grace,
In the tender glow of her luminous face.

Crickets chorus in a melodious ring,
As the wind carries tales the stars softly sing.
Wrapped in the warmth of lunar delight,
We sway to the rhythm of the quiet night.

Dreams tiptoe softly on pathways of light,
Guided by beams that shimmer so bright.
In her embrace, we find strength to stay,
While shadows retreat and fears fade away.

Oh moon, sweet muse, in your arms we belong,
Together we dance to your gentle song.
In the stillness of night, love finds its way,
As we dream and wander, till the break of day.

Dreams Entwined with Night's Mystique

In the velvet depths where shadows play,
Dreams entwine softly, night guiding the way.
A tapestry woven in midnight's embrace,
Where mysteries flourish, time leaves no trace.

With each little sigh, the stars seem to wink,
Inviting our souls to pause and to think.
Whispers of stardust dance in the air,
As we journey together, without a care.

The gentle night calls, with an echoing song,
Entwined in its magic, we know we belong.
Each heartbeat a promise, each moment a chance,
As we chase our dreams in a celestial dance.

Under the spell of night's mystique,
We find a connection, our own special peak.
In the embrace of darkness, we boldly ignite,
Our dreams dancing free, in the vastness of night.

Star-Kissed Verses of the Night

The stars twinkle softly, a distant choir,
Whispers of dreams, lifted higher.
Night's cool breeze wraps around me tight,
A canvas of shadows, painted with light.

Underneath heavens, my thoughts take flight,
With glimmers of hope in the hush of night.
I wander through galaxies lost in my mind,
Finding the secrets that the night has aligned.

Each star a story, each moonbeam a song,
Guiding the heart where it truly belongs.
In this celestial dance, I find my way,
Embraced by the silence, I long to stay.

Awake in the stillness, adventure calls,
Among the soft echoes, I hear the thralls.
In star-kissed whispers, my spirit ignites,
Journeying forward through magical nights.

Blossoms of Sleepless Wonder

In gardens where shadows linger long,
The blooms speak softly, a secret song.
With petals unfurling, the night they greet,
In the hush of the twilight, their fragrances sweet.

Awake in the stillness, imagination soars,
While moonlight envelops, unlocking the doors.
Each blossom, a story, a world yet unknown,
A tapestry woven from dreams overgrown.

The night paints the petals with soft silver hue,
As stars watch in silence, the sky vast and blue.
In the dance of the evening, a symphony plays,
Of blossoms that flourish in mysterious ways.

Sheltered in shadows, my thoughts intertwine,
In this sleepless wonder, your presence is mine.
Together we wander through dreams that ignite,
As blossoms of wonder unfold in the night.

Hushed Yearnings Beneath the Night Sky

In the twilight's embrace, we softly reside,
Where whispered yearnings and dreams coincide.
Beneath the vast canopy, hearts gently sway,
In the depth of the night, where secrets can play.

Moonlight caresses, a tender caress,
With stars giving witness to our sweet finesse.
In shadows and starlight, our stories are spun,
As we navigate paths where lovers have run.

Each breath shared in silence, a promise conveyed,
Beneath the cool heavens, our fears start to fade.
With hope as our blanket, we dream and we sigh,
In the hush of the night, where true feelings lie.

The cosmos above us, a guide to the heart,
In this moment together, we'll never depart.
With hushed yearnings echoing through the dark sky,
We find in the stillness, our spirits can fly.

Melodies in the Moonlight's Embrace

Notes of the night float on silken air,
Each moment a melody, simple and rare.
In moonlight's embrace, we sway to the tune,
With shadows as partners beneath the bright moon.

The whispering winds play our love's sweet refrain,
In gardens of stardust, we dance through the pain.
With hearts beating softly in rhythmic delight,
We lose ourselves gently in the velvet night.

Every glance is a chord, every touch a refrain,
In the concert of dreams, our spirits unchain.
As music of whispers envelops us whole,
The moon sings a lullaby deep in our soul.

With harmonies lingering in star-speckled skies,
We find our own symphony as night softly flies.
In melodies woven through shadows and light,
We cherish the moments crafted in night.

Night's Gentle Embrace

The moonlight spills like silk,
Casting dreams on sleepy eyes.
Stars twinkle softly in the dark,
As the world breathes a sigh.

Whispers in the gentle breeze,
Cradle the night in tender tones.
Shadows dance beneath the trees,
While the heart finds its home.

Time slows down in twilight's hue,
Wrapped in a sweet siren's call.
Memories linger like morning dew,
As night's embrace covers all.

A hush lands softly on the earth,
Where peace and calm intertwine.
In the stillness, dreams find birth,
Under the bright celestial sign.

Soft Lull of the Starry Veil

Beneath the stars, a gentle hush,
Nights drip with soothing grace.
The universe holds its breath,
In this sacred, endless space.

Dreams waltz in riotous colors,
With stardust weaves that intertwine.
The heart beats slow, the world drifts,
Lost in a celestial design.

Moonbeams peek through velvet skies,
A lullaby wraps the night.
Soft echoes of laughter and sighs,
Cradle the fading light.

In the quiet, all is possible,
Hope sings softly like a dove.
Wrapped in serenity's embrace,
The starry veil is a sign of love.

Twilight's Sweetest Soliloquy

As day bids farewell with a sigh,
Colors blend in soft retreat.
A symphony of silence swells,
Under twilight's tender heat.

The horizon blushes with glee,
While shadows stretch and sway.
Whispers of the evening breeze,
Led by dusk's sweet ballet.

Stars emerge like scattered seeds,
In the garden of the night.
Each one tells of hidden dreams,
Awaiting the morning light.

Listen to the twilight song,
Carried on the gentle air.
Time moves slow, where we belong,
Finding peace without a care.

Echoes of Sweet Dreams Beneath the Moon

Beneath the moon's watchful gaze,
Sweet dreams take their flight.
Whispers dance through the stillness,
Casting spells on the night.

Soft shadows cradle the earth,
In a blanket made of night.
Each twinkle in the sky's expanse,
Guides souls with quiet light.

In the stillness, hearts align,
With the rhythm of the stars.
The world fades in tranquil grace,
Wrapped in celestial bars.

Echoes of laughter linger near,
As the moon climbs high above.
In the silence, dreams draw near,
Bound in the arms of love.

Silken Shadows and Starshine

In the night, where whispers play,
Silken shadows softly sway.
Stars above, a distant choir,
Guiding dreams in gentle fire.

Lunar beams like silver lace,
Embrace the night with tender grace.
Echoes linger, soft and light,
Painting tales in quiet night.

Glimmers dance on tranquil streams,
Cradling all our secret dreams.
In the hush, where shadows dwell,
A world spun from a silken spell.

Hold my hand, let silence reign,
In this realm, we feel no pain.
Underneath the starry sky,
Together, we shall softly fly.

Hushed Echoes of the Twilight Breeze

Whispers float on twilight's breath,
Hushed echoes of the day's slow death.
Softly falling, shadows blend,
Where the night begins to mend.

Fingers trace the fading light,
Gather dreams that take their flight.
In the stillness, hearts will yearn,
For the lessons dusk will learn.

Gentle winds hum sweet refrains,
Carrying love through ancient plains.
As the last sun bids adieu,
We find solace in the blue.

Breezes weave through trees that sigh,
Painting secrets in the sky.
In this moment, time will freeze,
Lost within the twilight breeze.

Celestial Cradles and Dreaming Eyes

In the cradle of the night,
Celestial wonders spark delight.
Dreaming eyes, like lanterns shine,
Guiding hearts through realms divine.

Stars like gems in velvet deep,
Cradle wishes, soft and steep.
In their glow, the cosmos sings,
Serenade of infinite things.

Whispers float on cosmic streams,
Where reality bends to dreams.
In this dance of light and shade,
Our visions intertwine, unmade.

Underneath the vast expanse,
Let us join the cosmic dance.
Hand in hand, with spirits high,
We will soar across the sky.

Harmonies of the Midnight Serenade

In the stillness of the night,
Harmonies take wing in flight.
Notes that weave through the cool air,
Entwined in whispers of a prayer.

Moonlight bathes the world in gold,
Tales of love and dreams unfold.
Melodies that softly blend,
On this magic, we depend.

Strings of fate, they softly play,
Guiding us along the way.
In the symphony of stars,
We'll forget our ancient scars.

Let the midnight serenade,
Embrace all we've yet to trade.
In this chorus, hearts align,
Together we will brightly shine.

Moonbeam Dreams and Feathered Night

In the hush of night so deep,
Moonbeams dance, whispers creep.
Feathers fall like gentle sighs,
Painting silver in the skies.

Stars awaken, soft and bright,
Guiding dreams with purest light.
In their glow, all shadows fade,
Hope ignites, fears are laid.

Clouds drift slowly, a lullaby,
Cradling wishes as they fly.
With each breath, the world feels hushed,
In the stillness, hearts are crushed.

So let the night embrace your soul,
In feathered dreams, we find the whole.
With moonlight weaving through our sleep,
In this moment, secrets keep.

A Symphony Beneath the Celestial Sea

Underneath the starlit dome,
Waves of music gently roam.
Each note drifts on the cool night air,
A melody both rare and fair.

Whispers echo through the trees,
Harmonies carried by the breeze.
The moon plays softly, overhead,
To serenade the dreams we shed.

Glistening waves, a rhythmic beat,
With every pulse, our hearts do meet.
Beneath this vast celestial sea,
Nature's symphony flows free.

So let us dance upon the shore,
Where dreams awaken, longing for more.
In this moment, we are one,
A symphony until the sun.

Cradled in night's Soft Embrace

Night descends, a gentle sigh,
Stars emerge in velvet sky.
Cradled softly, shadows play,
Whispers weave in dreamy sway.

The moonlight spills like liquid gold,
Stories of the night retold.
In the stillness, peace abounds,
Safe in dreams where love resounds.

Kindred spirits whisper low,
In the dark, their hopes do grow.
With each tick of time's embrace,
We find solace in this place.

So close your eyes, let worries cease,
In the night, discover peace.
Embrace the quiet, breathe it in,
Cradled in dreams, let life begin.

Murmurs of the Midnight Sky

Murmurs rise with the evening breeze,
Secrets shared among the trees.
In the midnight's softest sigh,
Hope takes flight beneath the sky.

Stars are sentinels, shining bright,
Guiding pathways through the night.
Each twinkle holds a story fair,
Of dreams pursued, of hearts laid bare.

With every shadow, whispers flow,
Glimmers of the past we know.
The world hushes, the night draws near,
In the silence, truth feels clear.

So let the midnight sky above,
Fill your heart with endless love.
In murmurs shared, we find our way,
Beneath the stars, we choose to stay.

The Nightingale's Secret Song

In the hush of the twilight glow,
The nightingale sings soft and low.
Under stars, her whispers play,
Secrets hidden in the sway.

Wings spread wide, she takes to flight,
Guided by the silver light.
Each note a tale, a love so strong,
A melody where dreams belong.

Through the branches, echoes weave,
A lullaby that bids us believe.
In the heart of the night, she offers grace,
A symphony in this sacred space.

Her song brings peace, a gentle balm,
In the darkness, a soothing calm.
Listen closely, the world may fade,
As the nightingale's serenade is made.

Enchanted Slumber in Moonbeams

In the cradle of the night, we dream,
Wrapped in moonlight's silver beam.
Stars twinkle like whispers of old,
Stories of magic quietly told.

Gentle breezes sway the trees,
Carrying secrets on the breeze.
In slumber's hold, the heart takes flight,
Dancing softly in the night.

Dreamscapes bloom like flowers bright,
Bathed in the glow of soft moonlight.
Here in the magic, all fears cease,
Finding warmth in peaceful release.

As morning approaches, dreams will fade,
Yet the night's magic will not evade.
In our hearts, the moonbeams stay,
Guiding us back to the dreams someday.

Echoes of Dreams in the Stillness

In the stillness, whispers rise,
Echoes of dreams beneath the skies.
Silent shadows dance and twirl,
As we drift in a slumber whirl.

Thoughts take flight on moonlit wings,
Carried by the peace night brings.
In this quiet, heartbeats blend,
Finding solace as dreams ascend.

Beyond the veil of twilight's grace,
In the silence, we find our place.
Lost in visions, time slows down,
Wearing night like a silken gown.

Dreams weave tales, both shy and bold,
In this stillness, secrets unfold.
As dawn awakens, the echo stays,
A tender imprint of moonlit ways.

Celestial Sighs and Starlit Wishes

Beneath the vast and starry dome,
We gather wishes far from home.
Celestial sighs drift in the air,
Carrying hopes, both light and rare.

Each star a whisper, a glowing spark,
Illuminating the shadows dark.
In the night, our dreams are spun,
Woven together, two become one.

With every heartbeat, wishes rise,
Dancing softly in the midnight skies.
In the quiet, the universe calls,
As starlit magic within us falls.

So close your eyes, embrace the night,
Let your spirit take its flight.
In celestial wonders, find your bliss,
In the glow of the stars, seal a wish.

Soft Echoes of Night's Embrace

Whispers dance in the cool night air,
Stars peek through a veil of dark,
Each breath a secret softly shared,
Life's pulse beats in the quiet spark.

Moonlight bathes the world in grace,
Casting shadows soft and light,
Gentle dreams begin to trace,
Across the canvas of the night.

A lullaby of crickets plays,
Nature's choir sings so sweet,
Wrapped within the night's warm sway,
Silence cradles all we meet.

With every heartbeat, time slows down,
As stars twinkle with ancient might,
In this vast and endless crown,
We find our peace under night's flight.

A Tapestry of Midnight Harmonies

Underneath a blanket sewn of dreams,
The night unveils her soft refrain,
Each star a note in silver beams,
A symphony of cosmic chains.

The moon, a lantern glowing bright,
Guides weary souls on paths unknown,
With gentle hands it cradles night,
And weaves the tales of time alone.

Branches sway with rhythmic grace,
As shadows play in sweet embrace,
Each breeze a whisper, soft and low,
In harmony, the world does flow.

Dancing lights in the velvet sky,
Creatures stir with hearts ablaze,
As melodies of night drift by,
A dance of dreams through endless haze.

Night's Gentle Caress

A hush falls softly on the land,
Crickets sing their evening song,
The world, in darkness, takes a stand,
In night's embrace, we all belong.

Stars sprinkle hope like grains of sand,
Each twinkle a promise to hold tight,
In the cradle of vast expanse,
We breathe in whispers of the night.

Silver threads weave through the trees,
Branches entwined in a lover's hold,
A gentle breeze carries the keys,
To secrets of the night untold.

With every heartbeat, shadows grow,
In twilight's charm, we come alive,
The magic of night begins to flow,
As dreams and stars together thrive.

Rhythms of the Quiet Universe

In the stillness, a pulse resounds,
Galaxies spin in graceful arcs,
The universe shares its silent sounds,
Each moment illuminates the sparks.

Nebulae swirl in colors bright,
Cosmic wonders beyond our reach,
Night stretches forth with pure delight,
The cosmos whispers as it teaches.

Planets hum their ancient song,
Orbiting in a waltz divine,
Echoes of time where we belong,
In rhythm with the stars, we shine.

The vastness wraps us in its arms,
Embracing dreams that drift and glide,
With every heartbeat, magic charms,
In the quiet, love and hope reside.

Celestial Slumbers Under Starlight

Beneath the blanket of dark skies,
Twinkling stars begin to rise.
Whispers of night gently unfold,
Dreams entwined in cosmic gold.

Moonlight dances on quiet streams,
Shadows weave through silken dreams.
Resting hearts in velvet night,
Guided by the soft starlight.

Crickets serenade the hour,
Nature's breath, a calming power.
In dreams, we soar beyond the sea,
Where every wish can set us free.

In slumber deep, the world we roam,
Celestial skies, our whispered home.
With every sigh, we float on air,
Under the starlit world, we dare.

A Dance of Ashen Light and Dreams

From ashes of the fading flame,
A dance of shadows calls a name.
In dusky hues, we find our way,
To dreams that flicker, bright as day.

Whispers float like leaves on breeze,
Carrying secrets through the trees.
Each step a memory softly spun,
As night enfolds, we become one.

The echoes of the past collide,
In this gentle, twilight ride.
Our hearts in sync, we sway and glide,
While dreams and ashes coincide.

In this embrace, the world ignites,
With ashen beams and dazzling sights.
Bound by the rhythm, alive and free,
We dance through realms of mystery.

Night's Diary of Dreams & Delight

In twilight's grip, the pages turn,
A diary of dreams we yearn.
Each whispered word, a story told,
In silver ink on sheets of gold.

Minds wander through the woven night,
Seeking solace in starlit light.
Memories blend like colors bright,
Painting visions of pure delight.

Echoes linger in the air,
Fleeting thoughts, we softly share.
In quiet moments, time does blend,
As dreams and reality suspend.

Night writes softly, secrets spun,
Under the moon, we're all as one.
In this diary, our tales reside,
A treasure trove where dreams abide.

Cosmic Rails of Soft Embrace

On cosmic rails, we glide through dreams,
Where stardust flows in silvery streams.
A melody plays in the inky night,
Guiding our hearts, igniting delight.

Each star a whisper, a gentle thread,
In the fabric of night, where silence is bred.
We travel far on this celestial ride,
With the universe vast, we can't hide.

Embracing shadows, we soar and spin,
In the depths of space, our journey begins.
With every heartbeat, the cosmos sways,
Wrapped in the warmth of timeless rays.

In this embrace, the world fades away,
As we journey through night into day.
Together we dance in the starlit embrace,
On cosmic rails, our souls interlace.

Reveries in the Moon's Caress

In the stillness of night air,
Under a silver glow,
Whispers of dreams take flight,
Where memories softly flow.

Stars twinkle like lost hopes,
Dancing in the dark sky,
Each flicker a gentle nudge,
Inviting the heart to fly.

The moon wraps the world in peace,
Casting shadows soft and light,
A canvas for fleeting thoughts,
Painting visions in the night.

In this reverie, I dwell,
Bound by the night's embrace,
Each breath a sacred secret,
Eclipsed in the moon's grace.

Whispering Shadows of Dreams

Shadows dance upon the wall,
Echoes of stories untold,
Carried by the night's soft breeze,
In whispers dark and bold.

A tapestry of starlit fears,
Woven in threads of gold,
Each flicker a promise to keep,
In silence, they unfold.

Dreams take flight on feathered wings,
Gliding through twilight's veil,
With a sigh, they float away,
Like ships with tattered sail.

In the shadows, secrets linger,
They beckon with a call,
To find the light within the dark,
And rise above it all.

Midnight Serenades: A Soft Reverie

Softly strummed, a lullaby,
As night wraps the earth tight,
Each note a gentle caress,
Guiding dreams through the night.

Beneath the stars' sparkling gaze,
The world fades into peace,
In this serenade of whispers,
All troubles find release.

Moonlit paths line the journey,
Inviting hearts to roam,
With every stride, a story sings,
Creating a sense of home.

At midnight's grace, we linger,
In moments pure and true,
A symphony of stillness,
With dreams in softest hue.

The Silence of Silver Beam

In the hush of the quiet night,
Silver beams softly fall,
Lighting the dreams long buried,
Echoing a silent call.

The world in a tranquil pause,
Wrapped in serene refrain,
Every heartbeat synchronized,
With the stars' gentle gain.

Murmurs of the past arise,
Cradled in secret pockets,
Each whisper a comforting touch,
Hidden in moonlit rockets.

This silver silence demands,
A moment to breathe, to feel,
In the stillness, all is known,
And the soul begins to heal.

Themes of Stillness in the Night

In the hush of twilight's grace,
Stars awaken, a quiet lace.
Whispers dance on the cool breeze,
Time stands still amidst the trees.

Echoes linger, shadows play,
Night enfolds the fading day.
Moonlight bathes the silent ground,
In stillness, peace is found.

Crickets sing their nightly song,
In this calm, we all belong.
Softly breathing, hearts unite,
Embraced by themes of night.

Dreamers linger, thoughts take flight,
Wrapped in themes of soft twilight.
In the dark, our souls ignite,
Finding solace in the night.

Dreamscapes in Moonlit Whispers

Underneath the silver glow,
Dreams are born, and wishes flow.
Moonlit whispers gently weave,
Stories told for those who believe.

Through the veil of sleep we glide,
Across the realms where dreams reside.
Stars cast shadows, soft and bright,
In this dance of pure delight.

Thoughts cocooned in soft embrace,
Finding refuge in this space.
Every heartbeat, every sigh,
Paints the canvas of the sky.

We drift in realms where hopes align,
In moonlit whispers, we entwine.
Each dream a thread, a delicate thread,
In the tapestry of night, we're led.

Echoing the Secrets of the Night

In the dark, secrets gently flow,
The night has tales only few know.
Echoes lingering in the air,
Whispers soft, as if to share.

Stars hold stories, ancient and wise,
Secrets hidden behind their guise.
In shadows deep, truth may unfold,
In hushed tones, the night is bold.

With every breeze, a secret sighs,
Moonlit beams are watchful eyes.
Nature speaks in tender ways,
Echoing the night's soft praise.

Gather 'round, let the silence share,
The night's embrace, a gentle care.
In every whisper, there's a light,
Echoing the secrets of the night.

Nocturnal Muse and Its Sweet Call

In the shadows, muses wait,
Guiding hearts to dreams of fate.
Nocturnal whispers beckon near,
Inviting souls to shed their fear.

Softly glows the moon's embrace,
Each ray a touch of velvet grace.
In the silence, words take flight,
Dancing on the edge of night.

Creativity blooms, as shadows blend,
In midnight's arms, we transcend.
With every note, the muse will sing,
In the night, our spirits take wing.

Hear the call, let your heart soar,
As dreams awaken on the floor.
With nocturnal muse, we align,
In sweet call, our hearts entwine.

Songs of Stillness Beneath the Stars

In the night where silence lies,
A symphony of twinkling skies,
Soft whispers drift on gentle breeze,
Nature sings her songs with ease.

Stars like jewels in velvet cloak,
Each a dream, a timeless stroke,
Beneath their gaze, the world stands still,
Hearts awaken, spirits fill.

Moonlight dances on the stream,
Cradling every fleeting dream,
In this realm of peace profound,
Magic whispers all around.

Mysteries wrapped in night's embrace,
In stillness, we find our place,
Songs of quiet, sweet and clear,
Underneath the stars we're near.

Embrace of the Dreamweaver's Glow

In twilight's embrace, shadows play,
Dreamweaver weaves as night turns gray,
With threads of wishes, soft and bright,
Coloring the canvas of night.

Beneath the veil of whispered dreams,
Soft sighs flutter like silver beams,
In the glow of hope's gentle fire,
Hearts unfold and souls aspire.

As starlight falls on sleeping eyes,
In dreams we soar, we dance, we rise,
Every heartbeat follows the flow,
In the embrace of the glow.

Awakening at dawn's first light,
We carry with us the threads of night,
Woven visions in our soul,
Carried forth, they make us whole.

Whispers of the Moonlit Night

In moonlit gardens, shadows glide,
Whispers linger, secrets bide,
Each rustling leaf, a tale untold,
In silver light, the night unfolds.

Stars bear witness to the dreams,
Flowing softly like soothing streams,
Cloaked in night's enchanting breath,
It cradles life, it cradles death.

Gentle silence hums a tune,
Underneath the watchful moon,
Each note dances on the air,
Whispers shared without a care.

Time stands still in this soft glow,
As hearts beat slow, and spirits flow,
In the presence of the night,
We find our peace, we find our light.

Dreams Cradled in Silver Light

In the quiet of the night's embrace,
Dreams are scattered in sacred space,
Wrapped in glow, they softly gleam,
    Cradled gently, like a dream.

Moonbeams spill like liquid silk,
Nurturing hopes as rich as milk,
Each a promise, bright and clear,
    Guiding wanderers ever near.

Through the shadows, visions spark,
    Illuminated in the dark,
Voices whisper from the past,
Tales of love meant to last.

In this silvered, starlit night,
Embrace the dreams, hold them tight,
For in their depths, a world awaits,
A journey born within the gates.

Whispers of the Moonlit Night

In the stillness where shadows creep,
The moon whispers secrets, a promise to keep.
Stars twinkle softly, like dreams in flight,
Crafting a tapestry of the serene night.

Winds carry tales from the ancient trees,
Rustling their leaves, echoing with ease.
Each sigh of the night speaks to the heart,
Binding us close, though we're far apart.

Beneath the silver glow, lovers unite,
Dancing in rhythms, under soft light.
Every heartbeat syncs, a gentle embrace,
Lost in the magic of this sacred space.

As dawn's approach paints the sky in gold,
The whispers fade softly, their stories told.
Yet in quiet corners, they linger and stay,
Whispers of the night will never decay.

Celestial Dreams in Soft Hues

Cradled in colors of twilight's grace,
Celestial dreams drift, a delicate lace.
Whispers of stardust flow through the air,
Wrapping the world in a moment so rare.

Sky's canvas blushes with hues divine,
Clouds weave the stories where night stars align.
In this realm where the heart knows no bounds,
Every heartbeat is lost in beautiful sounds.

Gentle moonlight bathes the earth below,
Kissing the trees with a silvery glow.
Nature sighs softly, a lullaby sweet,
In celestial colors, our souls gently meet.

As slumber descends with its quiet embrace,
Dreams take flight in this enchanted space.
With every dawn, new hues will appear,
Celestial wonders, forever held dear.

Serenade of the Silver Sky

Beneath a silver sky, whispers arise,
A serenade trembles, soft as the sighs.
Melodies float through the cool evening breeze,
Carrying notes that put the spirit at ease.

Stars twinkle above, like a scattered tune,
Dancing in harmony, under the moon.
The night air shimmers with secrets untold,
A symphony rising, timeless and bold.

As shadows stretch long, the world starts to dream,
Every heartbeat resonates in one seam.
Glistening echoes of laughter and cheer,
Wrap us in warmth, holding loved ones near.

With each gentle sigh, the night softly fades,
Yet the serenade lingers, its magic cascades.
Even in silence, its song will remain,
A melody cherished, free from all pain.

Nocturnal Cradle Songs

In the arms of night, a cradle does sway,
Nocturnal melodies gently play.
Stars twirl and spin like children in flight,
Singing sweet songs through the endless night.

Moonbeams drape softly over dreams that unfold,
Kisses of starlight, worth more than gold.
Each note is a whisper, a promise anew,
Binding our hearts in a love ever true.

Crickets keep rhythm, their orchestra plays,
While the world drifts softly in slumber's embrace.
Gentle as feathers, the night takes its hold,
Rocking the earth in a story retold.

As dawn peeks with warmth, the cradle will cease,
Yet the echoes of night bring a whisper of peace.
Nocturnal songs linger like dew on the grass,
Treasured in memory, through ages they pass.

Echoes in the Blanket of Night

Whispers float on the cool night air,
Stars twinkle like secrets laid bare.
The moon watches over, a guardian bright,
Casting silver shadows, a dance in the night.

Footsteps fade on the silent ground,
In the stillness, soft echoes are found.
The heart beats slowly, in rhythmic delight,
Lost in the magic of the blanket of night.

Dreams weave tales in the woven dark,
Where wishes ignite like a tiny spark.
Time slips softly, like sand through our hands,
In the comfort of night, each moment expands.

As dawn approaches with gentle grace,
The night retreats, leaving a trace.
Yet in the shadows, forever shall stay,
The echoes of night, as night slips away.

Under the Canopy of Celestial Dreams

Beneath a tapestry of stars so bright,
Dreamers gather in the cool of the night.
With whispered hopes and wishes set free,
We chase constellations, you and me.

Clouds drift softly, a serene embrace,
As the universe sings at a gentle pace.
Together we weave through the cosmic glow,
In search of wonders, our spirits flow.

The air is thick with the magic of lore,
Each star a story, forevermore.
Guided by starlight, we feel alive,
In this realm where our dreams can thrive.

When the night fades, and dawn breaks anew,
The dreams we shared remain ever true.
For under the canopy, forever we'll find,
The celestial echoes that spark in our mind.

Hushed Tales Beneath the Twilight Sky

In the dusk's embrace, the stories unfold,
Of whispered legends and fables told.
Beneath the twilight, where shadows dance,
We gather round, lost in a trance.

The trees stand tall, guardians of time,
Keeping secrets, in silence, they rhyme.
A breeze carries tales from days long past,
Each breath a memory, forever to last.

Crickets serenade the coming night,
As fireflies flicker, a charming sight.
Together we listen, with hearts open wide,
To the hushed tales where magic resides.

In the fading light, old worlds collide,
With dreams intertwined, and souls as our guide.
For beneath the twilight, in the calm we embrace,
The whispered stories create a warm space.

Moonbeam's Gentle Blessing

The moonlight spills like a soft caress,
A touch of magic, a sweet, soft press.
In silver hues, the night is painted,
Each shadow softened, love untainted.

As moonbeams dance on the silken lake,
Ripples shimmer, a path to take.
With every glance, the world grows bright,
Wrapped gently in the embrace of night.

Dreamers wander, hearts open wide,
Guided by light, the moon as our guide.
In its glow, we find our way,
Through the quiet, the night becomes day.

So here we linger, in moon's tender glow,
With stories to share, and love to bestow.
For in moonbeam's blessing, dreams find their flight,
And hearts remember the magic of night.

Milton Keynes UK
Ingram Content Group UK Ltd.
UKHW020736301124
451807UK00019B/801